Clouds

Trudi Strain Trueit

Watts LIBRARY

Franklin Watts
A Division of Scholastic Inc.
New York • Toronto • London • Auckland • Sydney
Mexico City • New Delhi • Hong Kong
Danbury, Connecticut

For William, who sees beauty in every cloud and everyone

Note to readers: Definitions for words in **bold** can be found in the Glossary at the back of this book.

Photographs ©: AP/Wide World Photos: 46 (J. Pat Carter), 13 top (Beth A. Keiser); Corbis-Bettmann: 40; Dembinsky Photo Assoc.: 2 (M.L. Dembinsky Jr.), 31 (Mark A. Schneider), 27 (Ken Scott), 32 (Scott T. Smith); Earth Scenes/Stephen Ingram: 34; Minden Pictures/Gerry Ellis: 43; Peter Arnold Inc./Schafer & Hill: 37; Photo Researchers, NY: 41 (Bourseiller), 18, 19 (David R. Frazier), 16 (Georg Gerster), 44 (François Gohier), 33 (Jim W. Grace), 6 (Tim Holt), 5 right, 36 (George D. Lepp), 30 (Pekka Parviainen/SPL), 25 (Geoff Tompkinson/SPL); Photri: 26 (Biedel), 13 bottom (Frank Siteman), 21 (Mike Small), 15; Ricardo Carrasco Stuparich: 8; Richard Carlson/www.pals.iastate.edu/carlson: 28; Stone: 5 left, 23 (Tom Bean), 14 (Charles Doswell III), 10 (World Perspectives); The Image Works/Bob Daemmrich Photos, Inc.: 38; Visuals Unlimited: 24 (Rick Poley), cover (Mark A. Schneider).

The photograph on the cover shows cumulus cloud formations over a canyon in Utah. The photograph opposite the title page shows mammatus clouds, which are sometimes associated with tornadoes.

Library of Congress Cataloging-in-Publication Data

Trueit, Trudi Strain.
    Clouds / Trudi Strain Trueit.
        p. cm.— (Watts Library)
    Includes bibliographical references and index.
    Summary: Explains what clouds are, what causes them, their various forms, and the different weather conditions they accompany.
    ISBN 0-531-11969-6 (lib. bdg.)   0-531-16217-6 (pbk.)
    1. Clouds—Juvenile literature. [1. Clouds.] I. Title. II. Series.
QC921.35 .T78 2002
551.57'6—dc21   2001033420

Contents

Fluffy clouds float over the Hudson River in New York.

Chapter One

Cloud Catching

Have you ever chased after a fluffy marshmallow **cloud** on a summer's day? Have you tried to snatch it out of the sky even though you knew you could never really grab it? Well, what if you could?

Villagers in Caleta Chungungo, a remote mountain village in South America, are doing just that. Caleta is one of the driest regions of northern Chile. Unlike its neighbors in surrounding valleys, Caleta gets very little water from the Andes River. The village used to haul in

Villagers in Caleta Chungungo, Chile, use large nets to trap cumulus clouds for much-needed water.

truckloads of water, which became too expensive. In the early 1990s, Caleta was on the verge of drying up when people began to realize that the answer might be right above their heads. Low-level **cumulus clouds**, called *chamanchacas* in Spanish, frequently passed over the mountain. What if the town could somehow tap the water inside these clouds?

With the help of scientists, the village constructed eighty-six nylon mesh nets, each one the size of a highway billboard. The giant panels were then set high on the mountain to "trap" the cumulus clouds as they floated by. The plan worked. When the clouds passed through the panels, droplets of water **condensed** on the mesh, combined to form larger raindrops, and then fell through the holes into a specially designed reservoir to be purified for drinking.

On a day with good cloud cover, one mesh web is capable of capturing 185 gallons (700 liters) of water. Cloud catching supplies Caleta with about 80,000 gallons (300,000 L) of water each month at one-fifth the price of trucking the water in.

The Mystery of Clouds

From early sky gazers, who created rhymes to remember cloud patterns, to today's **meteorologists**, who rely on **weather satellites**, people have been fascinated by **nephology**, the study of clouds. At any given moment, clouds blanket at least half of our world. They reflect sunlight into space to help cool the planet. They also absorb heat from Earth and send it back down to keep us warm. Until recently, these airy plumes made of air and water were thought to be of little use except in predicting tomorrow's **weather**. New research, however, is showing that clouds are major factors in the quality of the air we breathe, extreme changes in weather, and the future of the Earth's climates.

In this book, we will discover how clouds take shape, from the calmest wisps of ice swirling high in the atmosphere to the deadliest of **tornadoes** rampaging across the Great Plains. We will seek out unique, rare, and dangerous clouds. Finally, we will learn how scientists are using the latest technology to unlock the secrets of clouds, our mysterious and ever-changing weather makers.

Weather vs. Climate

Weather is what is happening in the sky today over a certain area. It is based on such things as temperature, cloud cover, wind speed, and rain or snowfall. **Climate** refers to the prevailing weather conditions of an area over a long period of time, usually thirty years or more.

Rain clouds form in the troposphere over Africa.

Chapter Two

Creating Clouds

From scattered tufts of white to gray blankets fanning across the horizon, clouds come in all shapes and sizes. Clouds are a mixture of air, tiny dust or dirt particles, and **water vapor**—water in the form of invisible gas. Most clouds begin and end within the **troposphere**, the lowest layer of our atmosphere, which reaches about 10 miles (16 kilometers) above the Earth's surface. Made up of 78 percent nitrogen, 21 percent oxygen, and smaller amounts of other gases, the troposphere is the only band of our 600-mile-high (960-km-high) atmosphere that can support life.

Above the troposphere, extending 10–30 miles (16–50 km) above Earth's surface, lies the **stratosphere**. The stratosphere has virtually no weather at all. It contains **ozone**, a form of oxygen that protects Earth from the Sun's damaging ultraviolet radiation. Beyond the stratosphere is the **mesosphere**, about 30–60 miles (50–100 km) in space, followed by the **thermosphere**, 60–300 miles (100–480 km) up.

The troposphere, or **weather zone**, shifts slightly from season to season. Since cold air is heavier than warm air, the zone gets smaller in the winter and larger in the summer. This means that clouds tend to form lower in the sky in wintertime and a bit higher during the summer.

Cloudbirth

Have you ever seen your breath on a chilly morning? The invisible water vapor in your breath is attaching itself to tiny particles in the air. This creates a visible cloud. What happens to your breath is similar to the way many clouds take shape in the sky.

Without water vapor, our sky would not be decorated with clouds. Water vapor makes up only about 4 percent of the atmosphere, yet it has a big effect on our weather. If all of the water vapor in the air were to condense and fall as rain at the same time, our entire planet would be covered in 1 inch (2.5 centimeters) of water.

Green Bay Packers Gilbert Brown, Santana Dotson, and Doug Evans see their breath as it condenses in the cold Wisconsin air.

Water vapor condenses into visible droplets when it reaches the dewpoint.

Air rises to form clouds in three main ways. The first is called **convection**. When the Sun warms the earth, it heats up pockets of moist air near the ground. Since warm, moist air is lighter than cool, dry air, these pockets of air, or **thermals**, begin to rise. As the air rises, the water vapor begins to cool by about 5.5° Fahrenheit (3° Celsius) for every 1,000 feet (300 meters) it rises. When water vapor cools to a specific temperature called the **dewpoint**, it begins to condense, turning into tiny droplets of water.

The water molecules latch onto particles in the air, such as bits of dust or dirt. Far too small to see with the naked eye, these particles are called **cloud condensation nuclei (CCN)**. As the molecules of water wrap themselves around CCN, visible clouds begin to form in the

Violent, cloudy storms can give birth to tornadoes. Shown here is a twister near Hodges, Texas.

sky. If there were no dust, dirt, ocean salt, pollen, pollution, or volcanic ash in our air, water vapor would have nothing to cling to, and clouds would not form.

Clouds can also form when cold and warm air masses collide. Because cooler air is heavier than warmer air, the warm air rides up and over the cooler air. If there is enough moisture in the rising air, clouds will form. In the United States, cool, dry air flows over the Rocky Mountains to meet warm, moist air riding in from the Gulf of Mexico. When these two air masses hit, dark gray, billowy thunderclouds often result. The most powerful thunderstorms, called **supercells**, can trigger some of the wildest weather on Earth—tornadoes.

The third way clouds are created is through a process called **orographic lift**. When an air mass hits a mountain, it is forced upward. Once the air has climbed high enough to cool to its dewpoint, clouds are born. On the windward side of a hill (the side facing the wind), these clouds often rain or snow quite heavily. The mountain shields the opposite (leeward)

Orographic lift creates filmy clouds as air passes over a mountain.

side to form a dry area called a **rain shadow**. Mount Waialeale, Hawaii, holds the world's record for the most rainfall: 472 inches (1,200 cm) each year. In the mountain's rain shadow, however, the prairie grasslands are so dry that even cacti cannot grow there.

Cloudburst

Only about one cloud in ten produces **precipitation**, meaning some form of rain, ice, or snow. Although clouds look lighter than air, a typical rain cloud weighs billions of pounds. How can clouds float when they are so heavy? The water droplets

Quick Clouds

Most small cumulus clouds remain in the sky for only about 15 minutes before **evaporating**.

A thunderhead releases a torrent of rain in Third Mesa, Arizona.

(or ice particles) are so tiny—about 0.001 inch (0.025 millimeter)—that it takes them a long time to fall. They travel at only 2 feet (60 cm) per minute, and even the slightest breeze can keep them afloat. When these microscopic droplets collide to form larger and larger drops, they become too heavy to

16

remain in the cloud, so they fall to the surface. It takes about one million tiny cloud droplets to create a single raindrop large enough to fall to Earth.

The temperature of the air determines whether cloud droplets fall as rain, snow, ice pellets, or any combination of the three. For instance, what begins as snow high in the atmosphere can turn to rain if temperatures closer to the ground are higher than the freezing temperature of water, $32°$ F ($0°$ C). Precipitation can also change if it encounters several layers of different temperatures. **Sleet**, or ice pellets, is formed when snow falls through a layer of warm air and melts, then falls through a pocket of air colder than $32°$ F ($0°$ C) to refreeze before finally hitting the ground.

Rain Gauge

Raindrops vary in size from 0.008 inch (0.2 mm), smaller than the head of a pin, to 0.25 inch (6 mm), about the size of a pencil eraser.

Stratus clouds stretch like a blanket across an Oregon sky.

Chapter Three

Reading the Sky

People have been studying the heavens for centuries, but it was not until the early 1800s that English naturalist Luke Howard perfected a system of classifying clouds. Howard used Latin words to describe the way clouds looked from the ground. He called high, wispy, feathery clouds **cirrus clouds** (*cirrus* translates to "curl of hair"). Low and middle clouds that blanketed the sky like sheets were called **stratus clouds** (*stratus* means "stretched out"). Billowy, puffy clouds

Cloud Altitude	Type	Characteristics	Forecast
High-level Clouds Above 20,000 feet (6,000 m)	Cirrostratus	Thin, white, milky, sheetlike	No rain or snow, but precipitation might be on the way
	Cirrocumulus	Small, puffy, white ripples	
	Cirrus	Thin, white, wispy lace	
Mid-level Clouds Between 6,500 and 20,000 feet (2,000 and 6,000 m)	Altostratus Altocumulus	Gray or white, lumpy Gray or white, like waves or cotton balls	Precipitation unlikely, but can signal rain or an afternoon thunderstorm on a hot, humid day
Low Clouds Below 6,500 feet (2,000 m)	Stratus Stratocumulus	Gray, sheetlike Light to dark gray, lumpy or wavy, covering the sky	Drizzle or light rain Precipitation unlikely
	Nimbostratus	Light to dark gray, sheetlike	Precipitation likely
Clouds of Vertical Development Any altitude	Cumulus	Light or dark gray, with large puffs	Usually fair weather, but in hot and humid conditions, showers possible
	Cumulonimbus	Dark, towering, plume- or anvil-shaped	Main thunderstorm-producing clouds; heavy rain or hail likely; tornadoes possible

were referred to as **cumulus clouds** (meaning "heaping" clouds). We still use Howard's classification system today.

Clouds are divided into four main groups based on their height above the ground. High clouds are given the prefix *cirro-*; middle clouds start with *alto-*; low clouds begin with *strato-*; and clouds of vertical development, which form in several layers in the sky, are called *cumulo-*. Cloud subcategories include *fracto-*, meaning "broken clouds," and *nimbo-*, a prefix for any cloud that produces precipitation (*nimbus* is Latin for "shower"). Learning all of the cloud names can be confusing because the Latin terms are combined to describe more than one hundred different cloud formations.

Soaring Cirrus Clouds

Near the top of the weather zone high in the troposphere, in temperatures as low as -80° F (-60° C), ice crystals form feathery cirrus clouds. These clouds are often blown into long streamers by strong westerly winds at above 50 miles (80 km)

Ice crystals form wispy cirrus clouds high in the frigid troposphere.

per hour, but because of their height above Earth, they appear to be barely moving. Cirrus clouds usually do not cover the sky and are not thick enough to keep the Sun from casting shadows. They are also called mare's tails, paintbrushes, or spiderwebs.

Cirrostratus clouds are so thin that you can often see the Sun or Moon through the haze of their ice crystals. The crystals bend light rays, which can make the Sun or Moon appear to be wearing a halo. Cirrostratrus clouds are a signal that rain or snow might be on the way in the next 12 to 24 hours.

Cirrocumulus clouds look like small puffs of cotton. They form through **wind shear**, the effect of winds that strengthen or change direction with height. A sky of cirrocumulus clouds is often called a "mackerel sky" because the clouds resemble fish scales. This is one of the most beautiful cloud formations to see at sunset, when the fiery oranges and pinks of twilight reflect off their wavy ripples. Because wind shear often occurs ahead of storms, a mackerel sky can mean rain is coming soon.

Blankets of Stratus Clouds

Mid-level **altostratus clouds** are usually white or light gray and often appear as waves or flattened-out lumps. You might be able to see a watery Sun through their fibrous strands, but the sunlight that breaks through them is not strong enough to cast shadows on the ground. These clouds often show up ahead of rain or snow.

Low-level stratus clouds usually cover the entire sky, much like a sheet across the heavens. They look like a layer of fog

> ### A Cloud by Any Other Name
>
> In France, cirrocumulous clouds are referred to as *moutons,* or sheep.

Shifting Skies

The sky can contain several cloud combinations at once. For instance, you might spot high, wispy cirrus clouds being over-taken by a low layer of bumpy stratocumulus clouds. See how many different kinds of clouds you can identify in the sky at once. The more layers of clouds, the greater the chance that the weather is about to change and rain or snow is on the way.

that cannot quite touch the ground. In fact, low stratus clouds can begin as fog that rises into the sky. Stratus clouds might bring a light drizzle but are not considered heavy rain clouds.

Nimbostratus clouds are mid- or low-level clouds found below 6,500 feet (2,000 m). They are dark gray and thick enough to block the Sun from view. Nimbostratus clouds bring light to moderate precipitation that lasts from several hours to more than a day. Visibility is often very poor, as fog and ragged **stratus-fractus clouds** often form at lower levels.

Stratocumulus clouds are low-level clouds that come in lumps, waves, or rolls and look as if they are lit from behind. Although stratocumulus clouds look threatening, they seldom bring rain or snow. These clouds can be a signal of colder weather to come.

Cottony Cumulus Clouds

Cumulus clouds usually have flat bases and fluffy tops resembling cauliflower. They float along separated by large stretches of blue sky. Cumulus clouds are one of the most amazing cloud formations since they can be peaceful or powerful, depending on what the winds are doing. Most cumulus clouds

Towering cumulus clouds bear a strong resemblance to cauliflower.

are associated with fair weather, but when strong upward air currents form, they can grow into giant cumulus towers. The clashing of warm and cool air can spark severe thunderstorms and, in some cases, tornadoes.

Cumulonimbus clouds, also known as thunderheads, are dark towers with smooth tops. They produce heavy rain, hail, or thunderstorms. Vertical cumulus clouds can appear at any altitude, with their bases nearly touching the ground and their tops reaching heights of more than 75,000 feet (23,000 m).

Altocumulus clouds are mid-level plumes that often appear as gray, puffy blobs. One part of the cloud is usually darker than the rest. The clouds might look like castles rising high into the atmosphere. The presence of altocumulus clouds on a humid summer morning is one indicator that an afternoon thunderstorm might be brewing.

Into the Fog

Fog is simply a cloud that cannot get off the ground. It is moist air that has cooled below the dewpoint and is unable to get

The top of a cumulonimbus cloud, or thunderhead, is shaped like an anvil.

Learning the Lumps

Hold your arm up toward the sky and point your fist at the clouds. Low stratocumulus lumps will be about the size of your fist; mid-level altocumulus cloud lumps will be about the size of your thumb; and high cirrocumulus clouds will match up to your pinky nail.

Mist-aken Identity

Contrary to common belief, mist is not rain. It is actually a very thin layer of fog.

aloft. Fog is often so heavy with water that you can pass your hand through it and collect droplets of dew on your fingers.

Clear, chilly autumn evenings create one of the most common types of fog, **radiation fog**. Radiation fog usually forms at night, when the heat absorbed by the Earth during the day is radiated, or sent back up, into space. The fog forms upward from the ground as moist air is cooled to its dewpoint by a layer of drier air above, giving birth to fog. Radiation fog can form between 3 feet (1 m) off the ground and about 1,000 feet (300 m) up. A thick fog that hugs the ground can cut visibility to as low as 10 feet (3 m). Radiation fog usually breaks up quickly in the morning, once the Sun begins to warm the ground.

While radiation fog usually forms overnight, **advection fog** occurs most often in the day, when warm, moist air blows into a colder area and hits its dewpoint. Advection fog is often seen along the west coast of the United States, where it forms over the Pacific Ocean and is pushed inland. This dense fog can cut visibility to near zero. San Francisco is often blanketed for

Advection fog rolls off the Pacific coast past the Golden Gate Bridge in San Francisco. It's another foggy day in the Bay Area.

Steam fog hovers over a lake in Michigan.

days by advection fog rolling in off the Pacific. Cape Disappointment, located on the Washington coast where the Pacific Ocean meets the Columbia River, is wrapped in heavy fog 30 percent of the time, or about 100 days each year.

Have you ever seen fog rising off a lake in the cool autumn air? This is called **steam fog**. It occurs when cold, dry air flows over warm water. The water evaporates, saturating the air with moisture to form fog. The bottom of this fog often hovers barely a few inches above the lake. When this occurs on the ocean, it is called "sea smoke."

Rain and snow create their own type of fog, called **precipitation fog**. As rain or snow falls into drier air, it evaporates. The water vapor increases the moisture in the air while also cooling the air, causing clouds to form. Usually, as soon as the precipitation ends, so does the fog.

Caribou Dew

During Alaskan winters, large herds of caribou can fill an entire valley with ice fog just by exhaling their warm breath into the frigid air.

*Some clouds
seem to have a
sense of humor.
This one has
taken on the
distinct shape
of a rabbit.*

Chapter Four

Strange and Rare Clouds

Sky gazing is a lot like watching an artist paint on a canvas. A cumulus blob can suddenly turn into the face of a ferocious tiger. From minute to minute, clouds are changing shape and structure. Naming clouds for the familiar forms they take is called **nephelococcygia**, a slang term coined from the word *nephology*. Some amazing photographs have been taken of clouds that looked like rabbits, birds, and even human heads. While not everyone can say *nephelococcygia*, everyone can do it.

This chapter looks at a few of Earth's most bizarre cloud creations.

Heavenly Clouds

If a cloud's legendary silver lining really did exist, it would most likely be shining from within a **noctilucent cloud**. These rare bluish-silver cirrus clouds, also called night shining clouds, appear to glow in the dark. This effect is caused by the angle of the sinking Sun, which continues to light the clouds well after sunset. Noctilucent clouds can form 50 miles (80 km) above the Earth in the mesosphere, higher than any other type of cloud.

Some scientists think that a noctilucent cloud's glow is a reflection of water vapor in the atmosphere. Others say it happens when the Sun illuminates ice particles with meteor dust inside. Carbon dioxide (CO_2) particles in the atmosphere might also help to create these stunning and unique clouds.

Like noctilucent clouds, **nacreous clouds** appear to glow after dark or just before sunrise. These silver, feathery cirrus clouds, also known as mother-of-pearl clouds, are best viewed in the winter months in polar regions when the Sun is

A noctilucent cloud covers Finland.

low. Nacreous clouds form lower in the sky than noctilucent clouds, from 12 to 19 miles (19 to 30 km) high. No one knows why they occur, only that there seem to be more of them in a west-to-northwest wind.

Dramatic crepuscular rays shine through broken clouds.

Crepuscular rays, sunbeams that appear to light a cloud from behind, are one of the sky's most breathtaking visions. Sometimes called Jacob's Ladders, these light and dark bands radiate from behind clouds at either sunrise or twilight during

Unlike most clouds, mammatus clouds form when air sinks.

spring or summer. As the Sun shines between broken or scattered clouds, it reflects off particles in the air called **aerosols**. The darker rays are shadows cast by the clouds on the particle-filled air. Almost any broken cloud can produce crepuscular rays, but cumulus clouds create the most dazzling effect.

Most clouds take shape out of air that is rising, but bulgy **mammatus clouds** are triggered by air that is sinking. As air inside a cumulus or cumulonimbus cloud begins to cool, it drops, forming clumps of baggy clouds on the underside of the cumulus cloud. Mammatus clouds can be tricky to read. Because sinking air sometimes indicates that a storm is winding down, mammatus clouds are often a sign that the worst is over. But occasionally, if wind shear is present, these lumpy clouds can warn of a developing tornado.

Kelvin-Helmholtz clouds look like peaks of whipped cream in the heavens. Their crested tops, which also can resemble ocean waves, are formed by strong winds pressing against the very tops of cirrus clouds. One of the most distinctive clouds, a Kelvin-Helmholtz cloud is rarely seen because it tends to disappear quickly, less than a few minutes after forming.

Mountain Clouds

In the same way that skipping stones make ripples in a lake, a mountain can make waves in the air. Often, the most unusually shaped clouds hover around mountain ranges. **Lenticular clouds**, also called cap, lens, or wave clouds, look like disks or lids. They have been known to fool people into thinking alien spacecraft were invading Earth.

Angelic lenticular clouds paint the sky in Nepal.

Lenticular clouds are a signal to airplane pilots to be cautious—turbulent air might be near. Sparked by moist winds flowing in from the Pacific Ocean, lenticular clouds can often be seen above the Sierra Nevada in California. The May 1980 eruption of Mount St. Helens in Washington State changed the pattern of the peak's domelike lenticular clouds. When the top section of the mountain blew, the airflow shifted, and the rounded-cap clouds turned into flat saucers.

Lens-shaped lenticular clouds, seen here above the Sierra Nevada in California, have been mistaken for alien spaceships.

Banner clouds often form downwind near the top of a mountain. They appear to be holding on to the peak like flags flapping in the breeze. Mount Everest in the Himalayas and the Matterhorn in the Swiss Alps frequently give birth to banner clouds.

Special Effects

Coronas are rings of light that make the Moon and Sun look as if they are wearing glowing crowns. Coronas occur when light passes through very thin clouds or fog. The water droplets within the cloud scatter the light, painting colorful rings around the Sun or Moon. Blue is the most common color, but sometimes green and red rings appear. You are more likely to see a corona circling the Moon, since sunlight can wash out the ring during the day. The more water droplets there are inside a corona, the brighter it appears.

A **halo** is a white or slightly colored ring that appears around the Sun or Moon. While coronas are created by water droplets, halos require ice crystals to form. According to ancient folklore, "A halo around the Sun or Moon means that rain shall come quite soon." This could be true, since cirrus

Seeing Triple

Sundogs, or mock suns, are optical illusions created by ice crystals. The crystals reflect sunshine to form mirror images on both sides of the Sun, so it looks as if there are three suns overhead. You are most likely to see a sundog on a clear winter day when the Sun is low in the sky. Make sure to shield your eyes!

High-level cirrus clouds create a halo around the Sun.

clouds, which contain ice crystals, mean rain or snow is likely within the next 24 hours.

Although the Sun looks white, it is really a range of six colors shining together: red, orange, yellow, green, blue, and violet. Rainbows occur when the Sun's rays shine through raindrops and are **refracted**, or bent. The rain separates the colors, so we can see each distinctive band. Since fog is a cloud that cannot get off the ground, the tiny water droplets within it can also refract sunlight. Fog droplets are so small—less than 0.005 inch (0.012 cm)—that they cannot completely separate the colors of the Sun as raindrops can. Instead, the colors overlap or combine again. This creates a glowing whitish-gray arch, aptly named a **fogbow** or cloudbow. Fogbows are a rare and eerie sight, almost like seeing the ghost of a rainbow. You are most likely to see one if you stand on a hill on a gray, misty morning.

A ghostly fogbow stretches over the Arctic waters of Norway.

A weather forecaster checks data in Austin, Texas.

Chapter Five

Reaching for the Clouds

Nearly every country in the world keeps a constant "weather eye" on the skies above our planet. Each hour, thousands of weather stations send surface readings to their National Weather Service offices. Meteorologists issue forecasts to the public, collect climate data, and share information on a global scale. Thanks to new technologies, forecasters continue to learn more about how clouds take shape and move.

GOES I-M, the new generation of satellite technology, provides half-hourly data on temperature, winds, moisture, and cloud cover.

Radar is one tool scientists use to explore clouds and track growing storms. Conventional radar sends out microwave pulses that bounce off falling precipitation. The signal sends information about the size, strength, and direction of a storm back to a weather station. **Doppler radar**, an extra-sensitive microwave beam, allows forecasters to peer deep inside a storm. Doppler can detect even the smallest particles within a cloud. It is used to spot wind shear, which can cause tornadoes. Radar has also helped pave the way for new cloud discoveries. For instance, scientists used to think stratus clouds were fairly flat in shape until radar studies showed some with towers topping them, much like cumulus clouds.

Forecasters rely on weather satellites for larger views of

Earth's cloud patterns and storms. The National Oceanographic and Atmospheric Administration (NOAA) operates geostationary satellites known as **GOES (Geostationary Operational Environmental Satellite)**. You have probably seen these satellite photos on your television weather forecast. About 22,000 miles (35,000 km) out in space, GOES appears to be stuck in one spot but is really moving. It matches the Earth's rotation to keep tabs on storms, erupting volcanoes, **hurricanes**, and even deadly forest fires. Together, two geostationary satellites can view about 60 percent of the world at once.

Polar-orbiting satellites circle the Earth over the North and South Poles, photographing the entire surface of the planet every 12 hours. The satellites use **radiometers** to measure the infrared energy, or heat, emitted by clouds. The instruments can also detect water vapor in the atmosphere, a crucial ingredient to developing storms. Some polar satellites are so sensitive that they can spot a 100-watt light bulb from their position

Orbiting Ash

The 1991 eruption of Mount Pinatubo in the Philippines sent an ash cloud into the stratosphere, where it circled the globe for two years. The volcanic ash filtered out sunlight and cooled the planet by as much as 1° F (0.6° C) until it was finally brought down by precipitation.

500 miles (800 km) up in the atmosphere. By determining the kinds of clouds that are being born, meteorologists can better predict the weather they will create.

Besides assisting forecasters in their day-to-day weather predictions, the information gathered by radar and satellites provides new clues about Earth's climate. Clouds not only bring weather but also help regulate temperatures on the ground. Low, thick clouds generally cool us by reflecting the Sun's rays away from Earth. High, thin clouds allow the Sun to penetrate the atmosphere and trap heat coming from the ground, so they are considered warming clouds. Thick, vertical clouds reflect the Sun's energy into space while also helping to trap warm air coming from the Earth. Overall, scientists believe that more clouds are cooling the planet than heating it. Only long-term studies will confirm what is really happening, however.

Terra, the flagship satellite of NASA's Earth Observation System (EOS), was launched in December 1999 to monitor the health of our planet. It is the first satellite specially designed to study how oceans, land, and life influence one another. The onboard instruments can take more than forty measurements within clouds, including their thickness and temperature. The Multiangle Imaging Spectroradiometer (MISR) can view clouds from nine different angles and in three dimensions. Over the next fifteen years, Terra will send back data to show how our climate is changing naturally, how humans are changing it, and what the future holds.

Life Support

Water vapor and clouds are responsible for 90 percent of the natural greenhouse effect that warms our atmosphere and makes life possible.

A Delicate Balance

Natural processes carefully control our atmosphere. Gases such as carbon dioxide (CO_2), methane, nitrous oxide, and water vapor help trap heat from the Earth to keep us warm. Without this **greenhouse effect**, our planet would be 60° F (15° C) colder than it is now. Earth would be covered in ice!

Scientists worry that pollution is upsetting nature's fragile balance, however. The burning of **fossil fuels**—mainly gasoline and coal—by cars, ships, planes, and factories is sending large amounts of CO_2 and other greenhouse gases into the air. This has caused a worldwide trend of gradual heating called **global warming**.

At a paper plant in the state of Washington, burning fossil fuels send plumes of pollutant-filled smoke into the air.

There is 18 percent more CO_2 in the air today than there was just 100 years ago. In the last 30 years alone, we have doubled the amount of CO_2 in the atmosphere. The United States is responsible for 20 percent of the world's greenhouse gas pollution—more than any other nation on Earth.

Vapor or condensation trails called **contrails** are the white streaks made by aircraft as they travel across the sky at high altitudes. Contrails are formed when the water vapor in

Frozen water vapor from airplane engine exhaust turns into man-made cirrus clouds called contrails.

engine exhaust turns to ice before it can evaporate, creating man-made cirrus clouds. Since these clouds are heat-trappers, scientists are exploring how contrails might also be contributing to global warming.

Controlling Clouds

As long as weather continues to control us, we try to control the weather—especially when it comes to rain. Since World War II (1939–45), scientists have been studying ways to coax clouds into giving up their water through a process called **cloud seeding**. In one method of cloud seeding, a weather reconnaissance crew flies over puffy cumulus clouds and releases silver iodide or dry ice (frozen CO_2) from the plane. Inside the cloud, the chemicals mimic ice crystals, reacting with water vapor to trigger rain or snowfall.

Studies have shown that silver iodide does produce extra rainfall when averaged over a seven-year period, but there is no conclusive proof that it works every time. When it does rain or snow after cloud seeding, scientists cannot be sure if the chemicals worked or if nature simply took its course. For now, cloud seeding cannot end a drought, but it might help

An Oklahoma cloud-seeding pilot stands behind flare burners that spray chemicals, or "seeds," into clouds to coax rain.

build up water supplies during normal years to prepare for the dry ones.

Hydroscopic salt flares are the most recent discovery in cloud seeding. In 1988, during a cloud-seeding research program in South Africa, scientists noticed a single cumulus cloud growing in the sky above a paper mill. They soon discovered that the paper mill was sending up tiny crystals of potassium chloride and sodium chloride (table salt) into the air. Because the two salts attract moisture, they were creating large water droplets inside the cloud. The mill was simply copying the way the ocean seeds clouds. Scientists in South Africa, Mexico, and Thailand have been dropping hydroscopic salt flares into clouds since the mid-1990s, and their initial findings are promising.

Cloud seeding is not without controversy. Some scientists question whether humans have the right to tamper with nature. Squeezing the water out of clouds over one area could very well change the precipitation levels in another. From the 1960s to the 1980s, the United States experimented with cloud seeding to try to take the punch out of deadly hurricanes. Project Stormfury was designed to seed growing storms in the Atlantic Ocean near the Caribbean Sea, where some of the most powerful hurricanes in the world take shape. The project's goal was to drain powerful clouds of their rain, thereby breaking up a severe storm or hurricane before it reached land. Northern sections of Mexico depend on tropical storms for much of their annual rainfall, however. In 1980, officials in Mexico claimed that cloud seeding by the United States was causing a major drought in their country. Soon after, Stormfury was brought to an end. Scientists claimed that the seeding had never really worked anyway.

More than forty countries around the world currently have cloud-seeding research programs, but so far only forces of nature can determine when, where, and how much precipitation will fall. Perhaps someday someone will discover the recipe for making rain. Until then, we are left under the spell of clouds: fascinated by their beauty, amazed by their power, and longing to learn more about their magic.

The Rainmakers

The state of Texas, which receives only about 30 inches (75 cm) of rain in an average year, pins its hopes on cloud seeding to provide water for crops, cattle, and drinking. More than one-quarter of the state is seeded at a cost of over $3 million a year.

Glossary

advection fog—fog that forms when warm, moist air is blown into a colder area and cooled to its dewpoint

aerosols—microscopic particles of dust, dirt, or pollution in the air

altocumulus clouds—mid-level clouds that look like cotton balls

altostratus clouds—mid-level, white or light gray clouds that look like waves or flattened lumps

banner clouds—flaglike clouds that form near the top of a mountain

cirrocumulus clouds—high-level clouds that look like small puffs of cotton

cirrostratus clouds—thin, high-level clouds made of ice crystals that create a hazy sky

cirrus clouds—high-level, thin, wispy clouds made of ice crystals

climate—the long-term average weather of a particular region over many years

cloud—a visible formation of water droplets or ice crystals in the air

cloud condensation nuclei (CCN)—tiny particles of dirt, dust, clay, salt, pollen, or pollutants onto which water vapor condenses to form clouds

cloud seeding—a process by which chemicals are sprayed into clouds in an attempt to cause rain or snowfall

condensation—the process by which a gas changes into a liquid

contrails—condensation trails made by airplanes when the water vapor in their exhaust creates cirrus clouds in the sky

convection—the process by which pockets of moist air are heated by the Sun and rise to form clouds

corona—a circle of light around the Sun or Moon, created by light passing through cirrus clouds

crepuscular rays—beams of light that illuminate a cloud from behind

cumulonimbus clouds—thick, dark clouds that can produce heavy rain, hail, or thunderstorms

cumulus clouds—clouds with flat bases and fluffy tops, usually associated with fair weather but able to develop into storm clouds

dewpoint—the temperature at which water turns from a gas into a liquid

Doppler radar—a weather instrument that sends out microwave pulses to track the intensity and movement of storms

evaporation—the process by which a liquid changes into a gas

fog—a cloud that forms at ground level and cannot rise

fogbow—a whitish-gray arch that occurs when sunlight shines through tiny fog droplets

fossil fuels—fuels, such as coal, oil, and natural gas, that emit sulfur dioxide and nitrogen oxides, poisonous gases that help create acid rain

global warming—the gradual heating of Earth due to increased amounts of gases released by the burning of fossil fuels

GOES (Geostationary Operational Environmental Satellite)—a weather satellite that orbits Earth at the speed of the planet's rotation to monitor storms, volcanoes, forest fires, and other natural processes

greenhouse effect—the natural warming of Earth by atmospheric gases such as carbon dioxide, methane, water vapor, and nitrous oxide

halo—a ring around the Sun or Moon, created by ice crystals

hurricane—a tropical cyclone with winds at or above 75 miles (119 km) per hour

hydroscopic salt flares—a form of cloud seeding in which potassium chloride and sodium chloride are released into a cloud to create rain or snow

Kelvin-Helmholtz clouds—clouds resembling ocean waves that are formed by wind shear

lenticular clouds—clouds formed by mountain updrafts; also called lens, cap, or wave clouds

mammatus clouds—bumpy clouds that form on the undersides of cumulus or cumulonimbus clouds

mesosphere—the layer of Earth's atmosphere that extends 30–60 miles (50–100 m) into space

meteorologist—a scientist who studies weather

nacreous clouds—glowing clouds that are similar to noctilucent clouds but form much lower in the sky

nephelococcygia—the naming of clouds for the familiar shapes they resemble

nephology—the study of clouds

nimbostratus clouds—low-level clouds that usually bring light to moderate precipitation

noctilucent cloud—a high cirrus cloud that, due to the angle of the Sun, appears to glow in the dark

orographic lift—the forcing of air up and over hills or mountains

ozone—a type of oxygen molecule in the stratosphere that shields the Earth from the Sun's harmful rays

precipitation—any form of rain, ice, or snow that falls from a cloud

precipitation fog—fog caused by rain or snow falling into a layer of dry air

radiation fog—fog formed overnight when the heat absorbed by Earth is sent back into space

radiometer—an instrument that measures the infrared energy, or heat, of clouds

rain shadow—the area on the leeward, or back, side of a

mountain that receives far less precipitation than the windward, or front, side

refract—to bend; in the case of rainbows, to separate the bands of color in light

sleet—ice pellets that form when rain or snow melts, then refreezes as it falls

steam fog—fog that occurs when cold, dry air flows over warmer water

stratocumulus clouds—dark gray, low-level clouds that seldom bring rain or snow

stratosphere—a weatherless band of atmosphere that lies above the troposphere at about 10–30 miles (15–50 km) above Earth's surface

stratus clouds—mid- or low-level clouds that stretch like a sheet across the sky

stratus-fractus clouds—broken clouds that often form underneath nimbostratus clouds

sundog—an optical illusion formed when ice crystals reflect off sunlight to create a mirror image on each side of the Sun

supercell—a strong thunderstorm that can spawn tornadoes

thermals—small pockets of moist air that, when heated by the Sun, rise to begin the cloud-formation process

thermosphere—the outermost layer of the Earth's atmosphere that lies 60–300 miles (100–480 km) above Earth's surface

tornado—a violently rotating column of air that extends from the clouds to the ground

troposphere—the lowest level of our atmosphere, extending about 10 miles (16 km) above Earth

water vapor—water in the form of an invisible gas

weather—the condition of the atmosphere at a particular time as defined by clouds, Sun, wind, humidity, precipitation, and temperature

weather satellite—an electronic device that orbits Earth, gathering information about weather systems to relay back to scientists on the ground

weather zone—the troposphere or lowest level of our atmosphere, where most weather occurs

wind shear—the effect of winds that increase in speed with height, change direction with height, or both

To Find Out More

Books

Barnes-Svarney, Patricia, and Thomas E. Svarney. *Skies of Fury: Weather Weirdness Around the World*. New York: Simon & Schuster, 1999.

Christian, Spencer, and Antonia Felix. *Can It Really Rain Frogs? The World's Strangest Weather Events*. New York: John Wiley & Sons, 1997.

Harper, Suzanne. *From Mare's Tails to Thunderheads: Clouds*. Danbury, CT: Franklin Watts, 1997.

Lyons, Walter A. *The Handy Weather Answer Book*. Detroit: Visible Ink Press, 1997.

Rubin, Louis D., and Jim Duncan. *The Weather Wizard's Cloud Book: How You Can Forecast the Weather Accurately by Reading the Clouds.* Chapel Hill, NC: Algonquin Books of Chapel Hill, 1989.

Videos

Clouds. Schlessinger Media, 1998.

Eyewitness Weather. Dorling Kindersley Vision, 1996.

CD-ROMs

Everything Weather, The Weather Channel, Bureau of Electronic Publishing, Parsippany, NJ, 1995.

Organizations and Online Sites

Cool Clouds
Department of Agronomy
Iowa State University
Ames, IA 50010
http://pals.agron.iastate.edu/carlson
Dozens of photos of amazing clouds in familiar shapes can be found at this Web site.

How the Weather Works
301 Creek Valley Lane
Rockville, MD 20850
(301) 990-9324
http://www.weatherworks.com
Find experiments, activities, photos, and answers to your weather questions at this Web site.

National Aeronautics and Space Association (NASA)
NASA Headquarters
300 E Street SW
Washington, DC 20560
http://www.nasa.gov
NASA's photo collection gives satellite views of clouds while exploring Earth, climates, and space travel. Link to NASA's Goddard Institute for Space Studies and the Goddard Flight Center to learn more about clouds and climate.

National Oceanographic and Atmospheric Administration (NOAA)
Office of Public Affairs
U.S. Department of Commerce
14th Street & Constitution Avenue
Washington, DC 20230
(202) 482-6090
http://www.noaa.gov

The NOAA Web site features more than twelve thousand weather photos, 3-D weather images, and links to various organizations, including the National Hurricane Center, the National Severe Storms Laboratory, and the National Climatic Data Center. NOAA's page for students has educational resources, activities, and weather links. You can also link to the National Weather Service office located in your city or region.

USA Today
1000 Wilson Blvd.
Arlington, VA 22229
http://www.usatoday.com/weather
From the publishers of *USA Today*, this Web site offers easy-to-understand weather facts, graphics, and other educational information. You can search for weather conditions around the world or locate the forecast for your city.

A Note on Sources

In my weather research, I relied on one of the most comprehensive sources for any amateur or professional weather watcher: the National Oceanic and Atmospheric Administration (NOAA).

I called upon several affiliates of NOAA, including the National Hurricane Center in Miami, the National Climatic Data Center in North Carolina, and the National Weather Service, which operates a local forecast office in Seattle.

NASA's Goddard Institute for Space Studies and the Goddard Space Flight Center were also helpful in providing information on climate and satellite technology.

I tried to read as much material as I could that relates to weather: books written for young readers, reference works, and true-life accounts like those recounted in Sebastian Junger's *The Perfect Storm*.

Focusing further on the topic, I read detailed works such as *Skies of Fury: Weather Weirdness Around the World*, by Patricia Barnes-Svarney and Thomas E. Svarney; *Watching Weather*, by Tom Murphree and Mary K. Miller; and Walter Lyon's *The Handy Weather Answerbook*.

I continually updated my files with newspaper and magazine articles, particularly from specialized publications such as *Weatherwise* and *Scientific American*. I also studied the research conducted by universities with departments in atmospheric science, such as Pennsylvania State University and the Center for Clouds, Chemistry, and Climate at the University of California, San Diego.

Finally, growing up in the Pacific Northwest has given me a window to some truly spectacular weather events. From the fog that rolls through the temperate Hoh Rain Forest in Olympic National Park to a rare tornado touching down in the apple orchards of the Yakima Valley, I have had the chance to experience the wonder and power of clouds firsthand.

—*Trudi Strain Trueit*

Index

Numbers in *italics* indicate illustrations.

About the Author

As a weather forecaster for KREM (CBS) TV in Spokane, Washington, and KAPP TV (ABC) in Yakima, Trudi Strain Trueit has traveled to schools throughout the Pacific Northwest to share the world of weather with elementary and middle-school students. She is the author of three other Watts Library Earth Science books: *Storm Chasers*, *The Water Cycle*, and *Rain, Hail, and Snow*.

An award-winning television news reporter, Trueit has contributed stories to ABC News, CBS News, CNN, and the Speedvision Channel. Trueit, who has a B.A. in broadcast journalism, is a freelance writer and journalist. She lives in Everett, Washington, with her husband, Bill.